Angels We Will Hear on High!

Angels We Will Hear on High!

Stories for Christmas

Arthur F. Fogartie

Geneva Press
Louisville, Kentucky

Acknowledgments will be found on page ix.

Book design by Sharon Adams
Illustrations by Brenda Sullivan

First edition

Published by Geneva Press
Louisville, Kentucky

This book is printed on acid-free paper that
meets the American National Standards
Institute Z39.48 standard. ♾

PRINTED IN THE UNITED STATES OF AMERICA

99 00 01 02 03 04 05 06 07 08 — 10 9 8 7 6 5 4 3 2 1

Library of Congress Cataloging-in-Publication Data
Fogartie, Arthur F.
     Angels we will hear on high! : stories for Christmas /
Arthur F. Fogartie.
          p.   cm.
     Contents: Angels we will hear on high! — A trip down
the hall — The work — In search of — A detour through
Desserville — Christmas eve with Ivan — Christmas on
"The Farm" — What a Christmas!
     ISBN 0-664-50042-0 (alk. paper)
     1. Christmas stories, American.   I. Title.
PS3556.026A82 1999
813'.54—dc21   98-56397

To Dad,
. . . the rock from which I am hewn and
the pit from which I am dug.

Contents

Acknowledgments

The quotation on page 1 is from "The Night before Christmas," by Clement Clarke Moore.

The lines quoted on page 62 are from "Sweet Little Jesus Boy," by Robert MacGimsey, copyright 1934 by Carl Fischer, Inc. Used by permission.

The quotation on page 63 is from "Félise," by A. C. Swinburne.

"Invictus," by William Ernest Henley, quoted on page 64, was originally published in London in 1908.

The words from "Humpty Dumpty," on page 64, are taken from *The Glorious Mother Goose*, selected by Cooper Edens, published by Atheneum Books for Young Readers, an imprint of Simon and Schuster Children's Publishing Division.

"Incarnate Love," quoted on page 66, is by Christina Rossetti.

The quotation on page 67 is from "The Rhino," by Ogden Nash, published in *Verses from 1929 On,* by Ogden Nash, copyright 1933 by Ogden Nash. This poem first appeared in *The New Yorker* and is used by permission of Little, Brown and Company.

Acknowledgments

The lines quoted on pages 68-69 are from "Christmas Eve Meditation," by Margaret Bruner. Used by permission of the Christopher Publishing House.

The lyrics from "What Is This Lovely Fragrance?," English text by Edwin Fissinger (page 84), are copyright 1981 by Jensen Publications and are used by permission.

The quotation from "A Song in the Heart" (page 86) is by the author's great-aunt, Irene Vance Olsen.

The words of "Once in Royal David's City" (page 78) are by Cecil Frances Alexander.

Angels We Will Hear on High!

he young man bounded into the room like a hyperactive, two-legged Labrador puppy, all feet and energy. His entrance was not theatrical but certainly memorable.

I don't recall his exact dimensions at the time, but his presence seemed enormous. And, from the first moment I saw him, I could hear Clement Clarke Moore's immortal line ricocheting in my head:

> . . . a right jolly old elf,
> And I laughed when I saw him, in spite of
> myself.

Nothing about the fourteen-year-old reflected age, except, as I would learn later, his soul. The spirit he carried proved ancient beyond measure, stemming from somewhere out of an epoch for which we all long but which few of us ever visit.

"My name's Shane. Who are you?"

Never mind I had on a suit and a tie.

> Never mind we were in a pretty serious meeting, all of us sipping our beverages very properly for fear we might slurp.

> Never mind the obvious twenty or so years' difference in our ages.

Never mind he'd just wandered in from some athletic or physical endeavor, which obviously involved the presence of a great deal of dirt.

"My name's Shane. Who are you?" Not rude, just a very direct question riding a massive subtext. "Since you're in my house with all these people I already know and since my parents are being nice to you, you must be someone I ought to meet."

And from that moment, we were friends.

Oh, I wasn't alone. Across the next few years I found out no one was alone if Shane appeared—at least not for long. Shane found everyone—the nerdy, the geeks, the pimple-afflicted, the socially challenged, the person standing dutifully in the corner, assigned there by the popular crowd. Shane found them and, if nothing else, pestered them into a relationship. Even if you never spoke, you stood in silence shamelessly accompanied by Shane's hulking shadow.

He grew into a strapping young man. A fitting description: *strapping*. Big, raw, and strong as an onion sandwich.

Work all day—dance all night—talk until your ears looked for a place to hide. He could hike for miles without complaint, and when the others collapsed at the campsite, he would be out searching for firewood. If after dropping his lure into the lake he did not receive an immediate nibble, you'd better hang on, because just after the curt announcement, "They aren't biting here," he'd careen across the lake with the boat at full throttle. It was like fishing with some manic, self-propelled Frisbee.

A restless bundle of enthusiastic energy, pulsating for release.

And he could hit a golf ball farther than any human being I've ever seen. Absolutely never hit it straight. If it got airborne, he seldom kept it on the course. Some national defense site undoubtedly picked up a few of his shots on radar as they crossed time zones, but Shane would just drop another, look over, and say, "Really crushed that one, huh?" and we'd move along.

Eighteen holes and twenty-five or so balls later—at a point where most players would be looking for some lake into which to submerge their clubs permanently—Shane would find one stroke among his one hundred or so over which to rejoice and then spend the rest of the time figuring out when we could play together again.

The following should tell you something of his personality. When he was about six or so, his little buddies had a come-as-your-favorite-cartoon-character party. Dozens of tykes sprang forth as Cinderella, Snow White, Superman, Mickey Mouse, perhaps even a He-Man or two.

Shane chose his hero instantly and arrived at the festivities complete with club and faux-bearskin suit. And, from time to time, or so the story goes, the miniature partygoers froze in solemn, and perhaps petrified, stillness as the cry soared over the merrymaking:

"Cap-tain Ca-a-a-ve Ma-a-a-a-a-n!"

🌸🌸🌸🌸🌸

Possibly the most revered occupant of Shane's house is Choco—a massive retriever whose sole purpose in life lies in attempting to escape at any and all times. Houseguests receive significant and frequent warnings regarding the dog's proclivity, and so, when I was outside one evening and heard the jingle of Choco's tags and realized he was loose due to my stupidity (how was I supposed to know he could open the screen door?), I determined it was my responsibility to recapture him.

Off I charged in hot pursuit, at night, in a relatively unknown neighborhood, chasing Choco down streets and through backyards and across basketball courts—barefoot. Choco would pause occasionally, look back as if to say, "Here I am, old, fat, out-of-shape Idaho man," wait until I was about an arm's length away, and then trot off as I lunged.

When I lost him in the stygian gloom, I followed the sound of his collar: *chink, chink, chink, chink.* Choco had a great time. I almost had a stroke.

I finally corralled the miscreant when he stopped to investigate a fellow canine. I triumphantly looped my belt over his head and around his size-nineteen neck and headed home. Choco didn't want to go. And when that apparently three-hundred-pound dog sat and growled, I decided it was, indeed, a lovely evening to sleep under the stars.

Actually, I was sort of glad for the rest. City boys like me don't go to the beach without shoes. My feet were on fire.

A Jeep pulled up and Shane's voice echoed through the darkness.

"Hop in, I'll take you home."

Before Shane finished speaking, Choco had nearly dislocated my shoulder pulling me into his beloved buddy's car.

"Thanks, Shane." Breath came slowly.

"Art, that was really stupid. Really nice, but really stupid. Choco always comes home after a while. Of course, if he didn't, I could always say, 'This is Art. He visited my house, ate my food, and killed my dog.'"

Shane's chuckle welled up from some deep cavern as if a slumbering giant had awakened from a century of sleep and finally caught on to a joke he'd heard a hundred years earlier.

According to legend, when he was studying the schematics for the most recent renovations of Hell, Satan threw the plans back at the engineers.

"Not *hot* enough," he bellowed.

"But, Your Lordship, this is the best we can do."

"I don't think so," thundered the Prince of Darkness. "I want miserable. I want intolerable. I want stifling. I WANT TULSA!"

The Oklahoma sun beat on us with intentional, July malice. The blazing ball refused to relent until we puddled like the Wicked Witch of the West in *The Wizard of Oz* ("I'm melting . . ."). I cowered in what little shade I could find. Shane scrubbed away.

"This van is filthy!" He could have washed it with the sweat pouring off his neck.

"Shane, take it easy, buddy," I cautioned.

"How'd you get it this dirty?"

"We hit every bug for 1,500 miles," I said.

Shane's shoulders bucked up and down. "That's a good one, Art. Every bug for 1,500 miles."

Four more quarters shot into the slot. Shane punched the Wash button again.

"This ought to do it," he predicted. "Then, I'll rinse, wax, and polish."

"You've been scrubbing for forty minutes," I wheezed. "Don't you think it'll be okay?"

"Not gonna do a bad job, Art. Your van needs to be clean. You've got to travel more, right?"

"Not if you don't mind giving up your bed and sleeping on the couch for the rest of your life."

"That'd be okay. Can you really stay? Do you think you could? We could play golf tomorrow."

Visions of surface-to-air missiles flashed through my mind.

"We've really got to go, Shane."

A brief frown. "Okay, but this is gonna be clean."

He disappeared again and the van wobbled. Every so often, the long-handled brush broke the roof line, spewing bubbles in some demented impersonation of *The Lawrence Welk Show*.

Three or four more dollars for the rinse cycle. But Shane got his money's worth. I got wet.

"Gotcha!" he shrieked.

"Geez-a-Pete, Shane! Knock it off!" I tried to sound angry.

"I'm sorry, Art." Apparently I was a better actor than I knew. "I was just fooling around. You looked awful hot. I took it off jet and put it on spray. Did I hurt you?"

"Shane, it's okay. Just kidding. No problem. Water felt good."

"Oh, okay." Back at it. That van got scrubbed in places it didn't know it had.

Wax, polish, and a brisk rubdown with a towel. Shane looked like he'd run the New York City Marathon.

"Okay, buddy." I slid behind the wheel. "How much do I owe you?"

"Nothing, Art."

"Shane, you spent ten or fifteen dollars washing this thing."

"Only quarters, Art. That's no big deal. I get all Dad's extras."

"Well, let's head over to the Stop and Go. What do you want to drink?"

"Nothing."

"How 'bout ice cream or a milkshake?"

"No thanks."

The light was red. I turned to look at him. "Shane, you've got to let me do something."

"Art, if you pay me or give me anything, then I haven't done anything for you. I like washing cars.

I'm good at it." He paused. "Tell you what—I'll make it your Christmas present."

We got to Shane's house and he jumped out. But before he went inside, he peered around the bumper.

"Art."

"Yeah?"

"Merry Christmas!" And he bounced indoors, his pockets clinking with the twenty or so extra dollars worth of quarters he would have spent if he needed them.

❖❖❖❖❖

Shane doesn't wash vans anymore. On Valentine's Eve, while typically paying more attention to having a good time and to enjoying his companions than to either automotive safety or the speed limit, Shane rolled his Camaro and went to live with God.

A tragedy, a waste, but not really a surprise. "Shane wasn't foolhardy," one of his relatives said. "He just went to heaven the same way he did everything else—fast. If some people hear the beat of a different drummer, Shane marched along with his own, personal brass band."

I hear his father's calm voice: "It's hard this year, our first Christmas since. . . . We keep running into reminders of Christmases past—cards, gift tags, favorite presents. But the Star still shines and we will follow.

"We will not substitute gifts for grief, but we have started a little tradition. On a trip to New

York last week, I bought an angel for Carolyn. We'll get one every year as a way of remembering our son and of saying thank you for the Christ Child."

And so the seraphic collecting begins. A new angel appears every year—perhaps a silver-winged archangel or a candle-bearing cherub. No one is exactly sure what will show up, but everyone is confident that whatever arrives will absolutely enhance and enrich life's joys—sort of like living with Shane.

The angels will come—one by one, year by year—haloed soldiers standing sentinel over the birthplace of Bethlehem's King. Their numbers will increase until, from their vantage point of coffee table or mantle, they will remind every observer of

> . . . *a multitude of the heavenly host, praising God and saying,*
>   *"Glory to God in the highest,*
>   *and on earth peace . . .*

Regardless of the quantity or appearance of the angelic aggregation, those who look upon the ever-expanding field of wings will actively remember an exuberant young man of limitless zeal and in-your-face affection.

And, some time during this and every subsequent Blessed Winter Season, the angels will sing another tune.

Perhaps it will sound during the wee hours when shepherds quake and youngsters strain to hear reindeer on the roof.

Perhaps only a mother or father or brother will perceive the soothing music.

Perhaps the chorus will harmonize so softly the melody will just fall captive to hopeful hearts.

Perhaps the new rendition will begin every year when the rookie arrival appears from a nest of wrapping paper.

But the ever-growing choir that will annually announce the good tidings of great joy will surely also take breath and croon together an anthem of a softer but no less triumphant key. They will join their voices in honor of a gentle giant who embodied the very Spirit of Christmas with buoyancy and grace by wearing himself out washing a visitor's van on a day of sunstroke and blisters.

Yes, the angels will sing.

> For to us a child is born.
> And you shall call his name . . .
> *Shane!*

Ethan Shane Woodard died on February 14, 1996. This story is dedicated to the Glory of God and to Shane's memory. God bless us, every one.

A Trip down the Hall

ave you ever had trouble getting into the Christmas spirit? I don't mean, have you ever gotten a little irritated at the dweeb who snatched your parking place—

or wearied of the hubbub—

or stood in the middle of a department store and barely resisted the urge to shout, "Will someone here please help me!"

No, I mean, have you ever just flat out looked at that big, red "25" flashing at you like a neon sneer from the December calendar and thought, "So what?"

Well, that was me.

Three and a half weeks into the season of pear-treed partridges and winter wonderland walking . . .

Nineteen days deep in December's jovial commercialism . . .

A mere six sunsets away from the annual Rape of the Sabine Evergreen which is our package opening . . .

Three burnt candles on the ole Advent wreath . . .

And I did not give a rip about "Glory to God," "Santa Claus Is Coming to Town," "The Littlest Angel," the Osmond Family's saccharine special, or any of it.

If you'd have asked me the problem, I couldn't have pinpointed it. Tired? Sure I'm tired, but who isn't? The schedule we keep approximates timetable aerobics:

Okay, now—one more party . . .

Make this another late night . . .

Oh, the mall, the mall—we haven't been to the mall in eight hours . . .

Pound that frame, make it burn, let's stress-test this old warhorse until he fairly falls over with the joy of holiday exhaustion.

Oh, there had been high points. The choir did a nice job with the Vivaldi—music from heaven— and for a moment or two, the cloud lifted and the coming of the Christ seemed a possibility, but less than twenty-four hours later, I once again felt the drain of Advent anemia.

I sat at my desk most of Wednesday morning and tried to figure out my malaise. I like Christmas. I mean, I really like it. I am the quintessential Yuletide animal. Secular or sacred, if it has anything to do with Christmas, bring it on!

After every single gift is bought, after all the lists have been balanced (you know, did we get the same amount for him as we did for her? Does everyone have five stocking items? No, no, the dogs don't get candy canes!)—after every family member is covered, after all that's well out of the way, you can absolutely count on me to bounce in with a haul of unregistered and unapproved presents that makes Santa's bag look like an antique Lone Ranger lunch box.

If I think you need it . . .

If I think you might like it . . .

If I want to play with it and have to give it to you so I can . . .

I am liable to buy it.

Doesn't have to be expensive—I watch the budget—it just has to be sort of neat.

Lists? Who needs 'em? I shop by pure instinct. It's a gift!

But it is not all Land's End catalogs and credit card slips. The religious aspects hook me, too. You might think I would weary of the Baby in Bethlehem bit; after all, it's what I do for a living. But, as corny as it might sound to you, whenever the organ begins to crank "O Come, all ye faithful," or as soon as the congregation hits that part in the carol where you take a deep breath and plow into "Gloooooooooooooooria (gasp) in excelsis Deo . . . ," every year, I feel the lump rise in my throat, and I wipe away a tear as inconspicuously as possible.

I love reading that old, old story. I have to read it on Christmas Eve from the King James Version—that's how I learned it:

And lo, the angel of the Lord came upon them,
    and the glory of the Lord shone round about them,
        and they were sore afraid.

I was eleven years old or so, I guess, before I figured out that the shepherds were not in actual physical pain—sore afraid and all.

But the old King James language somehow makes the frayed and tender story come to life in a very special way, the story of . . .

Joseph, "of the House and lineage of David,"

And Mary, "his espoused wife, being great with child . . . "

The travelers going to Bethlehem because of Caesar Augustus, from whom "went out a decree . . . that all the world should be taxed . . . when Cyrenius was governor of Syria."

These familiar characters take on flesh and blood. They become real, and no matter how inaccurate my vision of the Holy Family may be, I can see them just as clearly every Christmas Eve as if they were standing next to me.

Joseph, a mountain of a man, quiet, strong, with huge, rough hands, completely unsuited for holding a baby; a little nervous, a little unsure, most certainly out of place, but steady and helpful.

Mary—have you ever doubted that she never wore anything other than a blue dress?—with a face of an angel and porcelain skin, the child mother of the child king, bringing the Babe into the world without protest (only Mary could do that), accepting the accommodations without complaint, receiving dirty, sheepy-smelling curiosity seekers with the elegance of a queen.

The story envelopes me with a strange and wonderful warmth. Whenever I hear the saga, I am six or seven once again, listening to the voice of my father booming across a darkened sanctuary, marveling in wide-eyed amazement at the miraculous appearance of angel choirs as if I were quaking on Shepherds' Ridge, all the while fidgeting with inquisitive excitement about what Santa would bring and trying to figure out exactly what it meant for Mary to ponder things in her heart.

Every Christmas, I grow young again, looking daily at a month that seems suddenly to expand by several days, that mocks my enthusiasm by moving the Big Event yet another few days off. And the closer Christmas comes, the more I find myself enmeshed in memories . . .

> . . . of a little brother who always cried after opening the package containing underwear—he thought it was a stuffed animal.

> . . . of sisters simultaneously giving raccoon collars to each other, and hugging and dancing all over the den like they'd gotten something really important like a football, while my brother and I marveled at their moronic behavior.

> . . . of the first time a young lady ever stopped by on Christmas morning to give me a present—my junior year in high school—and the absolute truckload of familial abuse that followed.

> . . . of the Christmas that someone, whose name I will not mention, learned why all those safety manuals tell you not to put

the branches you clip off the tree in the fireplace—the neighbors finally came over to warn us after they figured out they were not seeing the Star of Bethlehem but twelve-foot flames shooting out of the manse chimney. Dad never, ever burned another Christmas tree part.

So, it was not fatigue blocking my appreciation of the Season, or a lack of special recollections. Nor was it the contempt of familiarity with the biblical story.

I noticed people seemed a little more belligerent this year. I bet not three salesclerks said, "Merry Christmas." At least twice after shopping trips, I examined my car very carefully, but never could find the sign that must have been on there somewhere, reading, "Please pull out in front of me at a high rate of speed."

And, as I browsed and shopped, I took time to pick up a copy of Amy Vanderbilt's *Etiquette* and tried to discover exactly when it had become socially acceptable to rip items from the store shelves,

    pillage through them,

      try on socks,

        yank buttons off shirts,

          steal pairs of dice from games,

            and generally ransack merchandise.

Amy remains silent on the subject.

As much as I love gift giving and getting, even I recognized the commercial frenzy of the season has bloated way past the point of manageability. Maybe I lost interest about two days after Halloween when some disembodied voice tried to get me to send off for the seventeen-volume record collection of Andy Williams's "Christmas Memories."

I think what really pushed me over the edge was the manger scene. There are all kinds, you know—

wooden,
china,
glass,
stained glass,
papier-mâché.

I've even seen little painted rock characters. I can handle the little cherub crèches—you know, the ones where all the figures have chipmunk cheeks and little tykes' faces, a ceramic Hallmark nightmare. But when I saw the bear manger scene, I think I lost it.

No lie—bears, little cast and painted figures of the Nativity.

Mary Bear,
Joseph Bear,
Baby Jesus in the manger Bear,
even Wise Bears from the East,

And in an obvious oversight of the laws of the animal kingdom, Shepherd Bears. I could just imagine the conversation:

"What happened to all the sheep, Yogi?"

"Gee, Ben, don't know. Say, you got an extra toothpick?"

To complete the heresy, the gift store people wanted ninety-five dollars for the aberration and seventy bucks for it in miniature. The Bears of Bethlehem. Just about the only thing worse would have been looking in the manger to find Bart Simpson.

Father forgive us, I thought. We simply do not know what we are doing.

And we don't care, I decided. Maybe that's what really gripes me. We just don't care. We're so involved looking out for ourselves, we not only ignore the holy, we steamroll it. We try to make a profit by sticking cartoon characters in the place of the King.

The buzz of the intercom interrupted my indignation:

"Someone came by to see the pastor. He's been here before."

"*Someone to see the pastor*"—office code for "someone needs help . . . wants a handout . . . is looking for rent money."

"I'll be right out."

"No, wait. It's strange. He borrowed a pen and went outside. Said he'd be back."

"Okay, let me know."

I had barely turned back to my desk when I got beeped again: "He's here."

"I'm on my way."

Fred stood in his usual place: just inside the bench so he could see if and when I was coming. Fred is a relatively new addition to our regular crew of folks. We have a coterie of ten or twelve who do their business exclusively with First Church.

Fred is a nice man, a little cocoa-skinned gnome of indeterminable age. Looks shorter than he really is, never completely stands up straight, always looks like he's a little afraid someone is going to hit him. They may have—hit him, I mean. He has boxer's ears, little crooked petals of cauliflower on either side of his head.

Fred is friendly, always polite, never hassles any of the office staff. He is shy, with just a hint of an Isiah Thomas impish gleam in his eye.

Sometimes Fred comes with Edith, his wife. Mostly he comes in alone, but he always shows up needy, like all the rest, always wanting something.

Most of the time, I don't mind trying to help. Lord knows, I would not want to be in their shoes, homes, or lives. The very few who lie—who try to take advantage—seldom, if ever, come back. Most of the routine returnees try very hard not to abuse the privilege. But the parade of the indigent had gone on nonstop ever since Thanksgiving, and as I said, I was hardly Father Christmas. Here, one more time, was someone looking for something— asking much, giving little—one more palm in the sea of outstretched hands that I had encountered everywhere from department stores to Church Street.

"Morning, Fred. What can I do for you?"

"Nothing, preacher. We just came by to see you."

Edith appeared from around the corner.

"Hello, Edith. Is there something you need?" In my heart, I knew they always needed something.

"No sir. We just brought you this."

Fred reached back to Edith, who handed him a white, cardboard cake box. I stared at the top, at the carefully drawn, open letters that had obviously been sketched with the borrowed pen.

I opened the box. A pastry about eight inches wide grinned at me from the bottom.

"We got lemon," Fred said. "We thought you'd like that."

The pastry was wrapped in plastic. It occurred to me that Fred knew someone in my position probably wouldn't consider eating anything given by someone in his position if it didn't look surgically sterile.

"We got 'em to wrap it, preacher. We wanted it to be fresh."

"Fred, I don't know what to say."

"Nothing, preacher. Edith and I are just grateful for everything you do for us. God bless you. Merry Christmas."

And they were gone.

I don't know exactly how long I stood there, but after a while, the amazement wore off enough to allow my legs to move, and I walked down the hall holding a $1.25 pastry given to me by a man who probably didn't have fifty cents to his name.

As I turned the corner to my study, all at once, it was Christmas, and I broke into a tune I hadn't sung since I was a little boy:

> Mary had a baby, yes Lord.
> Mary had a baby, yes, my Lord.
> Mary had a baby, yes Lord.
> The people keep-a-comin'
> And the train's done gone.

> Called the baby Jesus, yes Lord.
> Called the baby Jesus, yes, my Lord.
> Called the baby Jesus, yes Lord.
> The people keep-a-comin'
> And the train's done gone.

> Laid him in a manger, yes Lord.
> Laid him in a manger . . .

The Work

t usually stands guard in the corner.
Tonight, however, it rests on my
knees, and I will tell what I was told.
But you won't understand any of this
without some explanation.

Exactly why I was driving across Kansas at
three o'clock on Christmas morning eleven years
ago is not hard to explain, but it borders on im-
possible to justify on any rational basis. Still, what
is rational about Christmas, especially when
you're twenty-seven and all by yourself on December 24th? So, when I decided at 7:00 P.M. in Kansas
City that the only place to be on Christmas morning was skiing outside of Denver, I packed my
stuff, loaded my skis, hopped in the Jeep, and was
rolling by 7:30.

The reports of inclement weather did not bother
me. I had chains and blankets in the back, a cooler
full of sandwiches and soda in the front, and my
trusty CB radio anchored under the dash. I'd be
okay. Didn't really zip along too much because of

the steady snow, but what the heck—I was going skiing. Sunshine is for Miami Beach.

What I hadn't figured on was fatigue. Climbing the ladder in a big law firm takes more mental stamina than muscle, but 350 miles down I-70, I suddenly felt someone had hooked cinder blocks onto my eyelids. I pushed on for another forty-five minutes on sheer willpower, but I knew I was going to have to stop.

Wakeeny . . . Quinter . . . Grainfield . . . Oakley . . . Each Kansas town a little smaller than the last and each with the same story I was well aware had greeted the most famous of all holiday travelers when they'd tried to get a hotel on Christmas Eve without calling ahead for reservations: *No Vacancy*. I checked out nine or so more places before I reached Brewster.

TRUCK S OP flashed the one-dead-letter neon sign, but it could have read *Live Alligator Farm* for all I cared as long as they had a bed.

"Sorry, buddy," the store clerk said. "We don't got a lot of rooms anyhow and some guy with a big rig on the way to Omaha just got the last one. He'd probably share, but I gave him a single and he weighs purt' near 290. You're outta luck."

Ever been so tired you felt like crying? My shoulders started to shake a little as I dragged back toward my car and I could feel the beginnings of tears in the corner of my eyes. I reached to close the door . . .

"Yo, buddy!"

The clerk sort of skated across the pavement. "Listen, ain't much, but there's a set of abandoned pumps out back. Area's well enough lit to be safe. I gotta be up tonight anyway, so I won't let nobody steal your tires or nothin', not that stuff like that happens much in Brewster. Why don't you pull 'round back and just sleep in your car? I'll wake you when I get off in the morning."

I guess I hesitated.

"No kiddin', buddy. I'll watch. Just remember to crack one of your back windows so your exhaust can't plug up on you and you'll be okay."

By that time, I'd have slept on one of the pumps. "Okay," I said. "Thanks."

"One more thing, buddy. If Ezra comes out, he's harmless. Nuttier than six boxes of Cracker Jack, but harmless."

Around the corner . . . stopped just outside the glare . . . cranked the back handle three-quarters of a turn . . . reclined the seat . . . jacket against the window . . . head on jacket . . . and out like a light. Oh, the irony was hardly wasted. My last thought had something to do with Mary giving birth and putting the Baby in the back seat of a Buick.

"Hey! Merry Christmas!"

Although the sun squinted over the horizon, it wasn't the rays that made me rub my scalp and blink; rather, it was the shooting pain from smashing my forehead into the ceiling when I bolted awake. Geez, that hurt, but not so much I didn't look around to see what had smacked into my window right next to my ear.

The voice erupted again: "Hey! Merry Christmas!" And, once more, the car echoed with what I now recognized as something rapping on the driver's window.

The face peering into the car defied age. Except for the closely cropped shards of white hair on either side of his ebony face, my caller could have passed for thirty-something.

"Hey! Merry Christmas!" He popped his walking stick against my window a third time. If I didn't answer, he might well just come through the glass.

My boot crunched the snow as I uncoiled from the car. "Morning," I croaked.

"Hey! Merry Christmas! You sleep out here, son? That's crazy. They say I ain't quite right—a little touched, if you know what I mean—but you won't find me snoozin' in no car."

"Uh . . . you have to be . . . uh . . . Ezra, is it?"

"That's me, son. They must've tol' you 'bout me. Let's see . . . nuttier . . . nuttier than ah . . ."

"Six boxes of Cracker Jack, I think is what he said."

Ezra snorted, "Yep, I heard that one. They think I'm squirrelly. May be, but I don't sleep in cars. It's okay, Randy," Ezra waved my vigilant night clerk back into the store. "I ain't botherin' him. You go on and work your last hour. I'm gonna shove some food into this young man."

Without another word he took me by the arm and headed me toward a corrugated metal building about fifty feet away. As an afterthought, Ezra yelled over his shoulder, "If I'm so crazy, how come you told him to sleep in the car?" Turning to me, he said, "And how come you listened?"

Pan-fried biscuits, country ham, sunnyside eggs, hash browns—served without so much as a "Would you like some?" Ezra just cooked, chuckling to himself occasionally while I wolfed my food. Everything washed down with coffee the consistency of motor oil, but, all in all, a fine breakfast.

"Hey!" I yelled in imitation after my fourth biscuit. "Merry Christmas!"

A smile twitched the corners of his mouth. "Merry Christmas back at you, son. Why you out in the car?"

"Nobody to spend Christmas with, so I decided to ski. I'm on my way to Denver."

"Lucky your car had plenty of gas—you could be an icicle this morning. If I'd have seen you last night, I'd have hauled you in here, but I sleep pretty hard. Anyway, got you filled up now."

"And I thank you, sir. How much do I owe you?"

"Don't make me slap you, son." Ezra stood erect—a tall man, dignified despite his obvious lack of formal education. "It's Christmas. No decent human being in the world makes another pay for Christmas breakfast."

"Well then, thank you. I guess I'll be taking off."

"Hey, Mr. Merry Christmas, not so fast. Didn't say there wasn't no obligation, just no charge."

"Excuse me?"

"You don't need excuses. You just got to help me with The Work."

"Say again?"

"The Work. The Work I do."

"Sounds fair," I responded. "What do you need—something moved or delivered or something?"

"And they call me crazy. I don't need help with my job. I can do most anything, and have. No, I mean The Work."

"Ezra, I'm sorry, I don't understand."

"Don't need to, son. Just sit down—there, where it's warm. Yeah, sit down and listen up. You'll be skiing soon enough."

Ezra pulled a stool close to the wood-burning stove, laid his walking stick across his knees, and leaned forward. He locked his eyes on mine—eyes dark, bottomless, magnetic.

"A long, long time ago," he began in a way that indicated the telling of a story he had memorized and recited many times, "long before our people came to this land in chains, one of my relatives, a man named Semonuttu, left his home in what is now Libya to learn about the world and to seek his fortune. He was the son of a proud family, an ancient line of warriors who had turned to thoughts of peace and prosperity.

"Before he departed, his father took him aside and gave him the sacred instructions. 'My son,' he said, 'when you return, bring with you a trophy from your greatest triumph.'

"Semonuttu, though adventurous, was a youngster of character, so he didn't seek out trouble. Instead, he tried his hand at different jobs in different places. After a while, he found he had a skill for trading.

"Now, his people had bartered and swapped for decades, but no one back home had ever made a living out of traveling from place to place doing so. Well, time passed, and Semonuttu found himself in a place called Carchemish."

Ezra paused as if to ensure I had kept up.

"Babylonian Empire," I said. He nodded and went on.

"So, he wandered all over the Old Testament country for years."

As Ezra spoke, he rubbed his walking stick with a soft, white cloth. The reddish wood glowed under his hand, warm and vibrant.

"Semonuttu went to Jerusalem a lot. The merchants there loved to trade with Nubians—that's what they called folk like you and me then, a term of respect. We were considered exotic. Anyway, on one trip to Jerusalem, Semonuttu saw the Great Sadness, found his greatest triumph, and right then and there, he quit the merchant business and headed home with his trophy. Other family members had theirs, but Semonuttu's was kept. Passed down it was, from father to child to child to child. Passed down 'cross time . . . 'cross the Mother Continent . . . 'cross the ocean . . . 'cross this country. Passed down all the way from Semonuttu to me, Ezra, to do The Work.

"Here it is—old Semonuttu's trophy!"

The staff hovered at my eye level, suspended only by Ezra's bony hands. The light from the open door of the stove made the walking stick shimmer.

"Heart of red cedar. That's what it is, son. Cut by Semonuttu's own hand. Been mine for nearly forty Christmases now. Only touch it twice a year. Once, when I oil it on the Day of the Great

Sadness, and the other on Christmas Day for The Work.

"Now you know, son."

Silence sucked most of the air out of the room. I sat there for a long time trying to understand the revelation I'd guessed I'd just received. When I finally spoke, I began slowly.

"Ezra, that's . . . ah . . . that's a nice . . . story. Does it mean anything?"

"What are you talkin' about, does it mean anything?"

"Well, you said a lot and it's interesting history, but the story doesn't tell me anything."

Ezra's head shook as he snickered. "You're gonna fly down a hill with two-by-fours strapped to your feet and they call me crazy. You're gonna listen to my story and ask 'Does it mean anything?' and they call me crazy."

His eyes turned to iron. "Son, have you been paying attention?"

"Yes sir."

"You go to Sunday school when you were young?"

"Perfect attendance for fifteen years."

"You go to college?"

"Phi Beta Kappa at Kansas, sir."

"Well, did you learn anything?"

"Sir?"

"What did they used to call New York?"

"New Amsterdam."

"What did they used to call Istanbul?"

"Constantinople."

"What did they used to call Iran?"

"Persia."

"West Asia?"

"Assyria."

"Israel?"

"Palestine."

"Son, what did they used to call the northern tip of Libya?"

"Uh . . . Libya was . . . uh . . . Cyrene. Oh, my God."

"That's right, son. I am a direct, living descendant of Semonuttu from Libya—known in his time as Simon of Cyrene.

"He toted The Man's cross all the way up the hill. Didn't think much of it at the time. You didn't argue with soldiers. Roman said 'Jump,' you asked, 'Can I come down?' Roman said, 'Carry that,' you said, 'Tell me how far to go.' But, after, when he was free to go, Simon stayed, and listened, and watched. He hung around the city, talking to folks, finding out more and more about The Man.

"And three days later, when what happened happened, Simon went back up on Devil's Hill. They'd left everything up. Didn't want to upset the citizens by working on the Jewish Sabbath. Besides, those crosses made pretty scary reminders about who was in charge.

"Simon knocked the frame over and cut a seven-foot piece of the vertical beam. He dragged it back down the very slope he'd dragged it up, took it to his room, and spent twenty-one days shaping his trophy. Then, when it was finished, he went home with this walking stick and started The Work.

"Get up off your knees, son. It's a stick, not The Man. Like the song says, 'O come, let us adore him.' We don't need this to worship—it only helps us remember. It helps us know that without The Great Sadness there wouldn't be The Great Joy. Without that, son, the shepherds just could have stayed in the field. If no one weeps in Jerusalem, no one ever hears the angels sing in Bethlehem.

"They think I'm crazy, son, but only 'cause no one here has understood yet. I just go from place to place until I find one person who will listen—and believe."

Ezra reached down and placed his hand on my head as if in blessing, "Hey! Merry Christmas!"

※ ※ ※ ※ ※

I enjoyed the skiing. It helped ease the loneliness of the joyous season. On the way home, I stopped in Brewster and knocked on the door of the shack behind the *TRUCK S OP,* but I wasn't particularly surprised when Ezra didn't answer. There wasn't even any smoke wisping out of the exhaust pipe. He had done The Work and moved on.

※ ※ ※ ※ ※

Two years ago, UPS showed up with a package. I never even bothered to figure out how he found me. The note inside was unsurprisingly brief:

> I have no family.
>   This is yours.
> You know the story.
> Now, do The Work.

It usually stands guard in the corner. Tonight, however, it rests on my knees and I will tell what I was told. The clean, white cloth gently caresses its luster and every time I begin, I hope my eyes grow as compelling as those of the Six-Boxes-of-Cracker-Jack man who taught me The Work:

> A long, long time ago, long before my people came to this country in chains, a man left his home to seek his fortune.

Hey! Merry Christmas!

In Search of . . .

ust settled over everything like the worn felt of an aging pool table. Attics get dusty, you know—the way people do. Dusty and crowded. You can only store so much in one place, be it the uppermost room of your house or the bottom of your heart, before circumstance, grief, lack of use, or neglect begins the inexorable job of coverage. Dust is to time what Pennzoil is to a V-6—it lubricates and makes it go.

And when you dare to stir, to poke, to investigate, to disturb, it rises like the tenants of a stomped-on yellow jackets' nest, the swirl starting about your ankles, up past your knees and waist, and then attacking the head in a desperate attempt to ward off the intruder. And though the sting of dust mites hardly pricks like the barbs of an angry hornet, I'd rather put up with a swollen hand than endure a teary-eyed, drippy-nosed, achy-headed allergy attack.

So, when I shuffled across the growling floorboards of my father's attic, the dust buzzed and swarmed and tried its level best to send me scurrying back to the relative safety of the pull-down ladder. But my knees groaned loudly from the trip up and the bruise on my scalp was rapidly developing the telltale characteristics of a lump after my forehead was so rudely and abruptly introduced to one of the roof beams, obviously before I could find the light. (I'd wax more descriptive about the four-and-a-half-watt bulb hanging in a totally idiotic and inaccessible position were this not a family story.) A retreat seemed more hazardous than moving forward.

I continued my glide through the semi-gloom, my six-foot, one-inch frame bent over to accommodate what I had learned far too late was a five-and-a-half-foot ceiling. I no doubt looked like one of the groveling servants from *The King and I*. Besides, I really couldn't go back. I'd been asked—well, not really. "Hey, Bozo, go to the attic and get the tree stand" hardly constituted an engraved invitation, but the mission had been assigned and a return to the decorating party (which roughly resembled the sacking of Troy) without the antiquated device that guaranteed at least one evergreen avalanche this evening would only mean another foray into this dingy land of throat-clogging grime and head-battering buttresses.

How much junk can someone collect? Didn't he throw away anything when he moved? Never ceases to amaze and confuse. *Geez-a-Pete . . .* box after box of books . . .

Enough lamps to open a Home Depot Lighting Center . . .

Hats and coats and bric-a-brac and, *hey, I've been looking for that . . .*

An overstuffed chair bleeding the contents of its overstuffedness through cracking seams and ever-widening torn places . . .

Jimmy Hoffa—no, that's a stuffed kangaroo . . .

A vintage television—*haven't seen a rabbit-ears antenna in a while . . .*

A wooden tennis racket.

Why in the world does anyone keep all this stuff? Tree stand . . . tree stand—"in the far lefthand corner in the big foot locker." Okay, north, south, east, left . . . ah, here we go . . . right over—YIKES!

I stood face to face with a pair of blue eyes that peeked out from under a shock of yellow-gold hair. Rosy cheeks supplied pink parentheses for a permanently pouted set of bright red lips.

Nancy! I almost shouted as soon as my heart restarted. Nancy, the life-sized baby doll. A gift to my sister from Santa oh-so-many—gosh, over thirty-five years ago. A marvel of doll technology somewhere around the time when the Russian Bear still prowled, Camelot set up shop in Washington, and before the Fab Four charged across the Atlantic to screams and swoons, Nancy appeared under our tree and took residence in my sister's room for—well, I guess until someone introduced a mandatory migration into the attic.

A simpler time, when one fifty-four-inch doll made a young girl's Christmas morning not only complete but also forever memorable. A happier, more innocent . . . *Ow! Ow! What the . . . ?*

The stabbing pain from my left foot might have reminded me of the folly of wandering through the attic without shoes had not it been overridden by the throbbing signals from the crown of my head I had just smashed into the ceiling when I straightened up to step off the . . . *What is that?*

A knight, medieval-type, molded plastic lance impaled in my sock, leered at me in triumph.

Sir Percival. How in the world, at age five, had I come up with a name like "Percival"? I was precocious, and the Round Table stuff really fascinated me, but in all honesty, Percy's name probably stemmed from a more mature—translated "aged"—and better-read source.

I sat, dust poofing from under my backside, and ran Sir Percival up and down Nancy's arm and remembered the Christmas both had come to join the family.

"Santa didn't have time to put this together," I recall Dad saying. And so we spent the better part of Christmas Day building The Dark Knight's castle—metal walls, plastic turrets, an actual drawbridge that would have worked if anyone in the room had held a degree in mechanical engineering. So, the gate sort of flopped around, which made it easy for Robin Hood's Merry Men to storm the place, but with horse-riding champions, sword-wielding heroes, brave archers, and a dapper king, who cared? We had a great time once Dad quit reciting Tennyson's *Idylls of the King,* and now Percival stood atop Nancy's blonde mop. "Excuse me, Milady, but did you know you were losing your hair?" And the knight shouted, "I, only I, am left!"

Creaking to my feet, I slipped the paladin into my pocket, wiped my hands on my pants and, like

Stanley, recommenced my forage through the attic jungle in search of Livingston's tree stand.

At least we needed a stand this year. The first Christmas after we'd arrived, about two decades ago, we were all grown but we still came home to this new and unfamiliar town during the holidays. Doc showed up at our door around the second week of December. "Let's go get a tree," he suggested.

Didn't really think much about it until we had driven several miles out of town and turned onto a gravel road with nary a tree lot in sight.

"I own a few acres. We'll find a good one here." Motioning to me, he said, "Grab the saw out of the back."

In our other existence, before we moved, when we still lived in the home of our childhood and adolescence—you know, the one in which Nancy and Sir Percival grew to maturity—someone had always delivered the tree. We'd come through the back door from school sometime in early December to the crisp smell of the forest and the awe-inspiring sight of a grand Scotch pine spreading its branches across our den, as if stretching its arms after a yawn.

But in the new life, which began well into our college years, in a new home and a new community, this new friend, Doc, determined we should adopt a new tradition—the quest. After walking for a while, my brother, being the more adventuresome—and at that point I believed the crazier of the two of us—spent the rest of the afternoon shinnying up forty-foot firs to see what the uppermost six or seven feet looked like. He would top one off, slide down, pick bark out of his chest, and we would assess. I bet he decapitated a dozen or so trees before we found something suitable.

What looks really good in the wild, however, sometimes lacks a little something in captivity. The tree was a tad sparse in places—shaded from the sun, I guess—but we made do and Doc promised a more successful hunt the next year.

Twelve months later, the chase inexplicably proved less flourishing. I guess Doc thought we were somehow to blame, tree-scalping rookies that we were, because on December 15th of year three, he faithfully delivered the tree on his own, unannounced. He came in, dragging the verdant carcass over his shoulder like a prize buck, and plopped it down in our playroom. "Already put a stand on it," he announced proudly. "Knew you wouldn't have time what with grad school and all. Merry Christmas!" Then he left.

A more pitiful evergreen specimen never even graced a Charlie Brown special. The poor thing exemplified the old golf adage of trees being 90 percent air, except we had a tough time actually finding the 10 percent tree part. When we clipped the angel to the top, the whole thing bowed as if in homage. I'd never seen a Christmas tree where the base and the tip both touched the ground at the same time.

Two days later, Doc's twenty-two-year-old daughter dropped in for a visit. An elegant young woman, she insisted on seeing her father's donation. With some reluctance, we led her to the scene of the crime. As soon as she saw "The Naked and the Dead," she burst into tears. "Yours looks so much better than ours," she sobbed.

The next year, Dad and my brother went to a corner lot at eight in the morning the day after Thanksgiving and paid somewhere around eight thousand dollars for a real tree—you know, a green one.

Tree stand . . . tree stand. There, over in the corner, the object of the pilgrimage: an old United States Navy footlocker. How we came to possess it defied logic. No one served in the Navy, but somehow, every attic needs a footlocker. Maybe it came with the house.

Off with the casual pillows . . . two suitcases . . . an aged Monopoly game . . . several armloads of magazines, the top one a copy of *Life* sporting a picture of "Abel and Baker," 1959 America's space-capsule-riding chimpanzees . . . some really unimportant stuff, down with the latches, up with the top.

Lying over everything, a dual-wire strand of Christmas lights, circa 1905 or so, wiggled like a bag of worms as the lid shook into the upright position. I laughed as I remembered the last year they graced the family tree, the last year they threatened the fire safety of the entire neighborhood.

My brother and I had finally achieved manhood. In Christmas terms that meant we were assigned the job the book of Leviticus apparently lays down as belonging to the dad: putting the lights on the tree. Though we've since learned that single act is probably what keeps both psychiatrists and divorce lawyers in business, at the time we were some hot stuff.

Did it all just the way we'd seen it done for years. Set up the tree; let the sisters scream that it wasn't straight; found the lights; laid out each strand lengthways across the den; plugged in every string one after the other, replacing any and all nonfunctioning bulbs with the exact same color because God help the poor idiot who desecrated the divinely preordained color scheme. Baby Jesus probably would refuse to appear if two red lights flickered next to each other.

Then, starting at the top and working down, with all the solemnity of the Magi bearing their fragrant oils, we placed wire on branch. After crowning the tree with the neatest and most venerated of all decorations—a plug-in angel with glowing wings—we stood back and turned on the pine-boughed objet d'art.

Every light perfect, every strand exactly positioned. And if you left the overhead light off and let the masterpiece twinkle by itself, you hardly even noticed the perfectly spaced, Christmas-tree-light bulb-shaped burns on the den carpet.

Don't need these, I mumbled, laying the combustibles aside. *I think they're illegal.*

The stand came out with a minimum of wrestling having hooked two of its legs under some sort of wax-encrusted log. I closed the trunk, snapped the latches, returned the astro-chimps to their rightful place, and turned for the perilous trip home.

A photograph clung to one of the legs of the tree stand. I perched on a barely uncluttered corner of the trunk, peeled off the picture, turned it over, and stared at one of the most beautiful women I have ever seen.

A luxuriously tiara-ed, statuesque brunette

gazed over the shoulder of her satin wedding gown, her face a perfect porcelain easel for her piercing, deep-set eyes. I'd seen those eyes a million times, dancing, laughing, expression-filled windows to the soul of a warrior-poet. The first feminist I ever knew, she spoke her mind not as much with her voice as with her life.

She had the physique of a cheetah and the heart of a champion. When focused, she played tennis with the killer instinct of a blood-sniffing great white or the piano with the precision of a Rolex.

Students flocked to her classrooms,
 travelers to her tours,
  and friends to her jet stream.

She could and would talk to anyone, but they had to move along with her. She sent notes to everyone. I could just see her hunched over her green-ribboned, Underwood typewriter, pounding out ninety-word-a-minute greetings, thank-you notes, messages of condolence, chatty correspondence, and gee-I-haven't-seen-you-in-a-whiles

Her internal radar could ping a lost sheep in any crowd, and you could bet your last nickel she would end up at every gathering talking for hours with the affair's social outcast, introducing every single person present to the individual she had found who previously hadn't known anyone, or driving someone home who did not have a ride. People awaited her entrance to a party simply because, once she was there, everyone knew they had a friend.

Her legendary energy shifted into overdrive the minute Thanksgiving dinner settled into leftovers. No one who so much as looked at her door during

December went away empty-handed. Didn't have to be much, but friends, acquaintances, neighborhood children, and delivery men all walked down her steps with something: a freshly baked cookie, a bag of peanut brittle, or one of fifty or so candy canes she kept in little Santa Claus boots hanging from a nearby banister. We all knew the next-door neighbor's kids rang the doorbell once a day, not because they cared if any of us wanted to play but just because she would give them a peppermint stick. She knew it, too, but didn't care. She handed out the confections anyway, every time.

Once she even grabbed a present from under the tree and thrust it into the hands of a surprised but grateful mailman who showed up earlier than she had expected. His gift sat not thirty feet from the door, on the dining room table, but it would not do to present anything unwrapped, so she peeled off the name tag and handed over a fastidiously prepared package, which turned out to be a little girl's makeup set. He gave it to his daughter, who was delighted and touched because, in those days, most white folks didn't give things to black postal workers. Oh yes, and when he came the next day, he found his gift waiting, wrapped in swaddling paper and lying in the mailbox.

Those in her house eventually learned everything was fair game, so presents had a way of hiding in secret locations until just before the family's Christmas Eve activities began. It wasn't that she hated shopping—she wasn't cheap—she just felt everyone ought to have something.

She was probably the first person from whom I

ever learned that the age-old story of a star, a mother, and a child slumbering in a stall was best reenacted and most suitably remembered by little rampant acts of kindness.

And from my first memory of the fire in her eyes until the day her optical embers ceased to burn, way too soon, she was the only person I've ever known for whom Christmas represented a 365-day-long event.

Merry Christmas, Mom. I stood again, wiped away a heartwarmed tear and headed for the ladder. And though the dusty floor still rampaged and I managed to hit my head three more times, the internal ache which gathers with the years subsided a little, my spirit felt a tad less congested, and I thought I heard the distant strains of "Joy to the World."

I must have presented quite a spectacle, standing there in the den, dingy tree stand in one hand, Nancy in the other, a string of fifty-year-old lights draped over my shoulders, and Sir Percival peeking out of my right-front pocket.

My brother laughed. "Where have you been, Bozo?"

"Got lost in the attic for a while," I replied.

"What have you been doing?"

I put down my load, unwrapped the electrical array from my collar, slid the photograph out from inside my shirt, and placed it softly on the coffee table.

Everyone smiled.

"Arthur, what have you been doing?"

"Not much," I grinned. "Just visiting Christmas. And doing a little dusting."

A Detour through Desserville

t δiδn't seem like Christmas. The
night air felt warm, even for a winter
evening in the South. Sort of typical
really—
of living below Mason and Dixon's demarca-
tion for thirty-five years,
of December 24th temperatures in the
mid-sixties,
of caroling door to door more often in
shirtsleeves than in sweaters.

You would think I would have grown accus-
tomed to the heat. But despite my love of the tem-
perate climate, deep down I longed for a chill in
the air and snow on the ground on Christmas Eve.

All day I had felt incorrectly dressed. I yearned
for a pair of khakis and a blazer. The longer I drove,
the more I imagined my wool suit pants were weld-
ing themselves to my legs. So, I journeyed down the
highway in the only non-air-conditioned car my
company owns, in an ever-increasing state of stick-
iness. Jack Frost definitely would not nip a single
nose within a hundred miles tonight.

My soggy situation might have upset me considerably more had I been in a hurry, or had someone

been waiting to meet me. I usually spend Christmas Eve with my sister and her family and have for as long as I care to remember. But this year, she had called me the day after Thanksgiving:

> Jack, Jack honey. I don't want to ruin your mood or anything because we've always been together, but it doesn't look like we'll be here for Christmas. Marvin and I have decided to go on a cruise. Well, you know, the last little one graduated in June, and we have some extra money, so we'll be in the Caribbean for two whole weeks. Won't that be grand? We wanted to depart later so you could join us, but then our travel agent—you remember Joyce Farrell, don't you?—well, she found a cancellation at about half the regular price that leaves on the 16th. I hate you can't go, but I know what the week before Christmas means to you sales-wise.

> Jack, I'm disappointed, but Marvin and I have dreamed about a trip like this forever. Are you going to be okay? We'll have Christmas with you the weekend we get back. Do you think you can make it by yourself? Are you sure?

What could I say? "Fine . . . oh yeah . . . great . . . I'm glad you can go. Yes, you've wanted to do this. I can stand to lose a few pounds, and you know I can't resist your pecan pie. I'll get some rest, watch a few ball games. You have a great time. Weekend after? It's a date. No problem. I'll see you when you get back." But my stomach knotted and my heart whimpered, "Please don't go. Please."

So I glided along the road, heading for an apartment that acted primarily as a rest stop and locker room in a city that was hardly a hometown.

If the occupants of the vehicle in front of me had not appeared so strange, I'd have never looked twice at the name of the town, much less remembered it: Desserville.

All of a sudden, I looked out of my windshield square into the back of an immaculately kept, antique pickup truck in whose bed bounced a most unusual assortment of folk:

a group of variable-sized angels,
a trio of fake-bearded wise men,
and two of the cutest little shepherds anyone ever saw.

Once I started to count, I just could not resist:

Four sets of wings,
Three Magi men,
Two shepherd boys,
On the road in the back of a Ford!

What a hoot! Nine biblically bedecked people bumping along, obviously on their way to the big annual bathrobe drama at their church. When the truck stopped at a traffic light, I admired the quality of the costumes. Someone had spent a lot of time making sure the get-ups looked first rate.

The truck paused for a while. I don't know why

because there wasn't any traffic coming. Some folk just can't seem to remember they can turn right on red.

Anyway, while I waited, I signaled "hello" to the gang in front. Everyone in the truck responded enthusiastically with waves and shouts of "Merry Christmas!" The driver finally woke up or something and made his turn, but he only went about thirty yards down the road and stopped.

Several sets of hands beckoned to me. The truck rolled on a few more feet, then halted again. Once more, an octopus of arms summoned me to follow, and someone yelled, "Come on, Mister, you'll never forget it!"

I sat at the intersection for a moment, debating. "Oh, what the heck? Nothing else to do," I muttered, and put the pedal down so I wouldn't lose them.

❦❦❦❦❦

"Evening, stranger! My name's George Simpson. Welcome to our pageant." Never have I encountered such an effusive church greeter. Simpson nearly pumped my arm out of its socket, but I didn't mind. It felt good to know someone was excited to see me.

Still clutching my hand, George led me up the stairs of the church. "Hope you like the service," he said. "We've really worked on it hard, added a few things this year."

"Has your congregation been doing this very long?" I inquired.

George beamed. I'd asked the right question. "Yes, sir, you bet! Every Christmas Eve since nineteen and fifty-five. That's the year we merged. Used to have three different churches in this little town, each scrappin' and clawin' for the few new folk who move in here. Always had been some talk of joinin' up, but in '55 it finally happened.

"We sort of threw the first show together. Seemed the way to go since none of the three churches had ever done a pageant before. Turned out to be a great presentation. Anyway, things went so well, we made it an annual event.

"Listen, we're gettin' ready to start. Just slip in the back over there and take the seat at the end of the pew. That's mine."

He caught someone's eye and motioned to them. After nods and gestures, George turned to me again. "It's okay. They'll let you have my place. No, no, it's fine. Always glad to have another guest. I'll go up and help the boys with the lights. Thanks for coming. Merry Christmas!"

❦❦❦❦❦

The familiar drama unfolded with tender precision, and from the opening moment the dedication of the good people of Desserville shown through.

Each scene followed the same format. While the minister read a passage from scripture, the actors made their way noiselessly to their marks on a darkened platform. As soon as the lesson ended, spotlights bathed the stage, revealing beautifully costumed characters frozen in place. With the appearance of each scene, the choir, stationed in the balcony, sang an appropriate musical selection.

I had seen a bunch of these things before. They're okay, but really, how many different ways can you dress up the old Mary and Joseph routine? Yet in all honesty, this one hit me.

One after another the tableaus unfolded:

> A bearded prophet stood before a quizzical crowd, his hands outstretched, his eyes burning with a desire for someone, anyone, to react to his summons: "A voice cries in the wilderness, prepare the way of the Lord. Make straight in the desert a highway for your God."

> Mary knelt before Gabriel, unsure of herself, yet confident in God, and the music lilted across the sanctuary, "Lo, how a rose e'er blooming."

> Joseph and child bride posed next to a rude manger, eyes cast down in admiration, or was it prayer?

> Once again, Gabriel, wings and arms spreading before terrified, eye-shielding shepherds (two of whom I recognized) while a bass voice thundered from the balcony, *"Go, tell it on the mountain, over the hills and everywhere. Go, tell it on the mountain that Jesus Christ is born."*

Scene followed scene. Maybe I was a little tired. Maybe the thought of a Christmas alone made me pay a bit more attention to the plight of a frightened family trapped in an unfamiliar place.

Maybe I just let the old, old story wash over me in all its elegant simplicity.

I don't know, but with every fresh vision, I grasped a little more of the Christmas miracle. I recognized with increasing clarity how the tale that took place "in those days" paralleled life in my own very contemporary world.

The saga began tentatively—young girls and carpenters and shepherds quaking, everyone a little unsure. Ordinary, everyday people caught in the whirlpool of God's action.

Others came with more confidence, attracted by the glitter and the noise: kings bearing gifts of a highly symbolic but uselessly extravagant nature. But soon these bigwigs found themselves slapped to their knees by the incomprehensibility of a new type of monarch: a servant king.

The pauper of a prince received them all, and still does . . .

from farm-hands to star gazers,
from auto mechanics to investment counselors,
from the illiterate to the brilliant,
from impoverished people speculating on the source of their next meal, to busy executives "doing power lunches" in their Savile Row suits,
from the watching and waiting ones to children too busy with their games and toys to take notice of a particularly brilliant star . . .

Everyone. The Child came for everyone—the little boy next to me so wired up about Santa he would not keep still; the woman in front whose expansive beehive hairdo partially obscured my vision; George Simpson, upstairs, getting in the way of the spotlight operators because he'd given his carefully saved seat to a stranger. The Babe came for them all.

And the Babe came for me!

When the organ sounded the familiar refrain, I fairly leapt to my feet to join in:

> Oh come, let us adore him,
> Oh come, let us adore him,
> Oh come, let us adore him,
> Christ, the Lord!

Muggy weather still reigned as I drove off, but somehow the heat seemed less oppressive. The miles passed faster now. I felt great, zipping down the highway, singing every single Christmas song I even suspected I knew, and I felt fortunate to have found those good and gracious people.

Thirty or forty minutes later, I stopped for gas. Thankful to find any place open at all, I filled up and went inside to pay.

The attendant didn't even look at me when he heard the bell. "Evening," he said. "That'll be thirteen and a quarter."

"Merry Christmas," I fairly shouted.

His head snapped back. "Say, you're chipper, Mister. Merry Christmas back at ya! Sorry if I was rude. Most folks haven't been very sociable tonight—forgot to buy batteries, or still had a way to go, or something. I only stay open so people can tank up. Probably lose a little money tonight, but who cares? It's Christmas Eve. Ought to try to help someone, right?"

"Well, I'm glad you're open."

He nodded appreciatively. "Thanks. Had a good evening, huh?"

"Yes, very nice. Very, very nice. Say, have you ever been to Desserville?"

The station owner broke into a broad, wistful smile. "Gee, Desserville. Not for a long, long time. Boy howdy, could they forevermore put on a show. Practically the whole town pitched in with the costumes, lights, scenery, whatever.

"Wonderful pageant. We used to get there an hour and a half early just to find a place to sit. My kids loved it. We went every year 'til I decided to keep shop on Christmas Eve."

He spoke with such warmth, I couldn't help myself. "Well, you said you're probably running at a loss. Why don't you start going again next year?"

A quizzical expression scrolled across his leathery face. "Not from around here, are you, Mister? Got a minute? Story's kind of involved. Well, if you're interested, sit down. Help yourself to the drink box. Need something to cool you off in that suit. Boy howdy, it's hot! Naw, put your money away. Merry Christmas!"

I popped the cap off a soft-drink bottle and leaned back in a cane chair. He spoke in a soft, slow voice.

"Yeah, it's hot all right. Matter of fact, it was a Christmas Eve just like this one I'm gonna tell you about—muggy, clothes sticking to you, felt like you couldn't quite get your breath all the way.

"It had been overcast and funny lookin' all day: big, heavy clouds with little tails and tinges of orange at the edges. Very strange. 'Bout four in the afternoon, it got real cool all of a sudden. Sort of gave you goose bumps, you know, and the sidewalks began to sweat something fierce. Water beaded up on 'em like someone turned on a spigot. That's always a bad sign. Storm watches all over. Everybody got a little skittish.

"Story I heard was a bunch of folk got together in Desserville to decide what to do 'bout the pageant. They went 'round and 'round like a cat chasin' his tail.

"Most of the old-timers figured everything'd blow over. They'd seen Mother Nature get her back up lots of times, and we'd never had much trouble. But, to tell the truth, I don't think anyone had to lean on anyone too hard. Fact is, no one wanted to call off the show—so much work, you know. People all excited, pulling together. They had hours, weeks in that production. And they knew they'd have a crowd. Naw, nothing in the world was gonna stop that pageant.

"Air warmed up a little near dinnertime, so everybody relaxed somewhat. They shouldn't have.

"'Round eight o'clock, the first funnel cloud touched down ten miles or so from where we're standing. Storm line traveled northeast, towards Desserville. By eight-thirty, tornadoes was poppin' in and out of the sky like ping-pong balls.

"Best anyone can tell, two or three twisters pogo-ed onto the Desserville church about eight-fifty. Place was packed.

"Another twenty minutes, everybody would have been gone, but wishin' don't make it so. Everything disappeared: sanctuary, people, cars, even the manger, vanished into thin air. Folk 'round here still haven't gotten over it."

I didn't say anything for a while. Finally, I broke the silence. "That's terrible. Lucky you weren't there. No wonder you don't go back."

He looked at me as if to question whether or not I'd been listening. "That's not the point, Mister," he said. "There's nothing to go back to.

"You see, the tornado hit Christmas Eve in 1966. There hasn't been a pageant in Desserville since."

Christmas Eve with Ivan

Very few, if any, of the people living on the street are there by choice. Not all of them are unintelligent or uneducated. Nor are all of them addicted to alcohol or drugs. Some live on the street because of bad luck or by chance. Others are there because some cataclysmic event shattered them and drove their lives downward in an inexorable spiral. This is the story of one such man.

 now! This is neat! Snow! Don't like it any other time—makes it too wet. But Christmas Eve needs it. Snow!

Needs lots of things—Christmas Eve, I mean— like peace on earth, and reindeer, and goodwill, and angels, and presents. A shepherd would be nice. No wise men, though—they didn't come 'til later. Ivan knows the story.

From the East they were—East . . . Asia . . . dark, strange men from dark, strange places bringing dark, strange gifts. Burial ointments for the Baby. *Ich!*

Ivan was a wise man once. No, not in the play. Ivan was the littlest shepherd boy in the church play. No, Ivan was a wise man. Lots of money. Lots of friends. Lots of things. *Let's do lunch . . . Tennis later? About two-ish? Ciao, babe.*

They came from all over to hear the wise man: *Better not do that now—bad timing . . . Invest over here . . . Double production there . . . Broaden this . . . Eliminate that.*

Ooooo . . . aaaaah! They all raised their eyebrows and stroked their chins. Ivan, the wise man.

Yep, that's what we need—snow. Christmas Eve needs snow and other stuff. Ivan needs new shoes. Wet goes right through the cardboard. But gotta have snow on Christmas Eve.

Bundle up the Baby, Mother Mary. Angels make him smile, but blankets keep him warm. Always watch the Baby. Babies need lots of help.

Snow, good snow, white and fluffy. Maybe it'll be dry. That'll keep Ivan's feet un-wet. Didn't have any good shoes for Ivan at the Shelter. Maybe New Year's. Folks'll get rid of their old shoes when Santa brings them new ones. Ivan will make it.

Ivan is Ivan because of Caesar, you know. Caesar called himself Caesar. Learned that in eighth grade—Mr. Spurrier's history. Sat next to Ricky . . . Ricky . . . Ricky Walker. Smart boy.

Ivan spent the night with him once during Christmas break. No tree. No stockings. No peppermint. Ricky was poor. Wore bad clothes—jacket with a hole in it. Poor . . . but happy.

Ivan ate dinner with them, and, afterward, they all sang. Took turns. They even made Ivan sing. Mrs. Walker had a wonderful voice. She sang "Sweet Little Jesus Boy." Hers was best. Ivan cried.

> . . . born in a manger.
> Sweet little holy child,
> Didn't know who you wuz.

We don't have many decorations, she told Ivan, but we've got each other and we've got the Baby Lord, and he always comes when we need Him. That's enough.

Ricky Walker . . . history class . . . Caesar was Caesar. Ivan remembered when Ivan got rich.

"Merry Christmas!" Ivan knows him. Works in Ivan's bank. Used to be Ivan's bank. "Yes, sir! No, sir! I'm sorry, sir! More coffee, sir? Merry Christmas, sir!" Oh, they treated Ivan fine. Ivan was a wise man.

Now, Ivan mostly sees the guards. They're nice. Ivan was always nice to them—tall, straight guards in blue suits.

Mother Mary wore a blue dress, you know. Blue chiffon. Matched her eyes.

Tommy had blue eyes—green and blue. They changed, dark and flashing. Ivan remembers the poem:

> Those eyes the greenest of things blue,
> The bluest of things grey.
> Eyes colored like a water-flower,
> And deeper than the green sea's glass.
> Eyes that remember one sweet hour—
> In vain we swore it should not pass.

Look into the Baby's eyes, Mother Mary. Look deep and hold on. They get sick, you know. They get sick, and weak, and inoperable, and they fade away. Far, far away.

Ivan's bank! The big one over there, built forty-five stories tall with Ivan's money. Ivan was a mover and a shaker. Ivan was a wise man.

Caesar was Caesar. Ivan is Ivan. Ivan lived the poem:

> Out of the night that covers me,
>   Black as the Pit from pole to pole,
> I thank whatever gods may be
>   For my unconquerable soul.
>
> In the fell clutch of circumstance
>   I have not winced nor cried aloud.
> Under the bludgeonings of chance
>   My head is bloody, but unbowed.
>
> Beyond this place of wrath and tears
>   Looms but the Horror of the shade,
> And yet the menace of the years
>   Finds, and shall find, me unafraid.
>
> It matters not how strait the gate,
>   How charged with punishments the scroll,
> I am the master of my fate;
>   I am the captain of my soul.

All roads lead to Ivan. Take it to Ivan; he can solve it. No problem too tough for Ivan. *And Ivan will reign until he has put all enemies under his feet. And the last enemy to be destroyed . . . is . . . Death.*

Not destroyed yet, you know. The Man with the Sickle is still out there. One at a time, he gets them all. He got Caesar. He got Mother Mary. He got Tommy.

> All the King's horses
> And all the King's men
> Couldn't put Humpty Dumpty together again.

That's right, Tommy. Very, very good. You learned that one fast. Let's hear another. You're so smart. Good boy.

How about a catch? Want to throw with your dear old dad? Okay, burn it in. No, no! That's low minors stuff. It's outta here—over the fence—a one-way bus ticket back home. Bring some heat!

Atta boy! That's your good stuff. Mow 'em down. Fourteen in a row. Way to go, Tommy!

That's my kid out there. 7–0 this year. Un-hit-able! Pitched the winning game in the high school state championship last year.

Look! Look over there—the guy in the hat! Yeah, the one with the clipboard—scout for the pros. Wants to talk to Tommy right after the game. They're gonna offer him a contract because he's the best they've ever seen.

> *Buy me some peanuts and Cracker Jack.*
> *I don't care if I never get back.*

No more baseball.
No more pro scouts.
No more Tommy.

What do you mean inoperable? Fix it! You transplant hearts, for God's sake. Do something. Help him. He's seventeen years old, for cryin' out loud! He's still got games to pitch, and hearts to break, and malls to cruise.

Ivan went to the mall the other day. Yes, Ivan goes to the mall. Ivan loves to look. No touching! Never touch! If Ivan touches, they think Ivan steals. Never, never touch!

So many pretty things . . . little dolls dressed like elves . . . Santa with a long line at his cardboard North Pole House. Excited children—running and laughing and pointing and asking—wonderful children. It's a happy time.

> Christmas is coming, the goose is getting fat.
> Please put a penny in the old man's hat.
> If you don't have a penny, a half-a-cent will do.
> If you don't have half-a-cent, God bless you!

Excited children . . . and angry parents. Why are they angry? Ivan even saw a woman slap her son. Slap! At Christmas! Pow! Right on the head.

Ivan doesn't speak to strangers. Scares them. But Ivan spoke to the slappin' lady.

Mother Mary didn't hit her boy. She wouldn't hit the Baby. The Baby's coming. Don't hit your boy or the Baby can't bring him to see you. Ivan never hit Tommy. Tommy comes.

Love that boy, lady. Love him tight. Squeeze all his love 'til it runs out. I loved Tommy 'til there wasn't any left. Christmas is not for hitting, lady. Christmas is for love.

Ivan told her all that 'cause Ivan knows the poem:

> Love came down at Christmas,
>   Love all lovely, Love Divine;
> Love was born at Christmas,
>   Star and Angels gave the sign.
> Love shall be our token,
>   Love be yours and Love be mine,
> Love to God and all men,
>   Love for plea and gift and sign.

The Security Man asked Ivan to leave. He was nice. He knows Ivan. Ivan just scares people sometimes.

You like Ivan's shirt? It's new. Got it the same place as last year: at the Big Church. Ivan didn't used to go there, not close enough to Ivan's big house. Now, Ivan lives downtown at the Shelter, so Ivan goes to the Big Church.

> Here is the church . . .
> . . . here is the steeple.

It has a big steeple, a huge iron finger that points to the Baby. It shows us where to look.

On the lawn of the Big Church they have a Stable—Mother Mary, Joseph, and the Baby in a box. Little Baby. Ivan guards the Baby. Ivan keeps him safe 'til the shepherds come to watch.

The Big Church feeds Ivan breakfast on the Sunday before Christmas—Ivan and two or three hundred of Ivan's friends. We all come in. It smells terrible. It smells like a zoo.

> The rhino is a homely beast.
> For human eyes he's not a feast.
> Farewell, farewell, you old rhinoceros,
> I'll look at something less preposteros.

Isn't that a funny poem, Tommy? Let's go look at the elephants. There's a silly poem about them, too . . .

Anyway, Ivan and his friends make the Big Church smell bad, but the people there are nice. They give Ivan soap, and a toothbrush, and a comb, and a shirt. Every year! It's soft because it's new.

And red! See! Red checks! Ivan's favorite. Bright, like Tommy's fireman's hat with the siren and the light on top. He ran all over the house on Christmas Day with the light blinding everyone and the *woo, woo, woo* all day.

Ivan finally took out the batteries. Told Tommy it was broken until later. Ivan hated the red fireman's hat. Now, Ivan misses the red fireman's hat.

See my red shirt? It's so pretty, Ivan put it on right then. Ivan went into the bathroom and changed. Ivan just threw the other one away. A whole year makes a shirt not soft anymore.

Ivan likes the manger scene at the Big Church. Mary's so pretty, and Joseph's so strong. But Ivan really likes the Baby. He's Ivan's special friend. Ivan stays with the Baby tonight—not at the Shelter like usual. Ivan lets someone else have Ivan's place. On Christmas Eve, Ivan stays with the Baby.

The police who watch the Big Church used to try to run Ivan off—"Get out of there!"—but Ivan explained it all, and now they understand and check on Ivan.

Don't cry for Ivan. Not tonight. It's Christmas Eve. It's Jingle Bells and Rudolph. It's Angels and little lambs.

Don't cry for Ivan. This is the best night of all. Tonight we all stay in the Stable. The Baby . . . Ivan . . . and Tommy.

Tonight, Ivan sees the Child, both of them.

Tonight, Ivan doesn't hurt anymore. You see, Ivan believes the poem:

There is a hush that comes on Christmas Eve—
Life's hurry and its stress grow far away;

And something in the silence seems to weave
A mood akin to sadness, yet we say
A "Merry Christmas" to the friends we meet,
And all the while we feel the mystic spell,
As if the Christ Child came on noiseless feet,
With something old, yet ever new to tell—
The eyes grow misty, yet they shed no tear,
And those that we have lost, somehow seem near.

Christmas on "The Farm"

otten. No other word accurately described the boys' attitudes, or their behavior, as a matter of fact. Not surprising though. What else would you expect during the Christmas season from a bunch of kids, aged eight to eighteen, with no homes, no families, and little, if any, hope?

The other boys and girls, the ones in school, breezed through December all happy and wishing, primed for the big payoff on the morning of the twenty-fifth. They all knew they'd find at least one unique gift, or welcome some special visitor, or something.

But the youngsters from the Milford County Home for Boys never dreamed. Why set yourself up for more disappointment?

The plunge in spirits and deportment hardly surprised Bill Boyd. He'd experienced the nose-dive annually in each of his twelve Christmases as director of "The Farm."

How the Home came by its nickname Bill couldn't recall, if he ever knew. Perhaps because of its rural setting, more likely because the "throw-back" facility tended toward the old ways—no group homes or cottage situations—so the kids moved in herdlike fashion from dorm to gym to dining hall. Anyway, everyone called the place "The Farm."

Bill didn't like the boys' twelve-month belligerence, but he'd learned to live with it. So, every single December, he sat by his office phone and fielded the inevitable calls from school.

Johnny pushed someone in gym . . .

Eric sassed his homeroom teacher . . .

This one skipped class . . .

That one broke a window.

They weren't bad kids—just, well, just unlucky, that's all. Different backgrounds and different stories, but every last one of them sharing one common ground: nowhere to go, no one to care.

Bill did the best he could, and largely succeeded. But, as soon as the lights and tinsel went up in homes and stores, The Farm's emotional barometer plummeted.

Early on, Bill tried different gimmicks to cheer things up: plays, movies, guest speakers, even a magician. Nothing worked. The kids recognized bone-throwing when they saw it.

So, the year after someone set fire to Presto the Astonishing's magic trunk, Bill trash-heaped his rose-colored-glasses crusade. Better just let them sort things out their own way.

And for the most part, they did.

The Christmas Eve routine had evolved into its own little ritual, almost unchanging from year to year. Turkey dinner at 8:00 P.M., lovingly prepared (if not well prepared) by Bernadette Grizwald:

part cook, part music teacher, part warden, part nurse, full-time target of ridicule.

After dinner, the gifts. Bill handed out his first. Books, always: Hardy Boys for the elementary aged, one of the classics for the junior and senior highs. Every year he longed to do more, but a paucity of funds and a generous discount at a local store annually added up to books. The guys always griped a little, ragged him about having "an old man's taste," but most of them read the volumes, and even those who didn't kept them on the shelves next to their beds.

His last official function of the evening always involved dispersing the packages from local churches. Before the subdued festivities began, Bill took time to remove the cards from the white-wrapped presents. He steadfastly refused to read: "Boy, age nine." But even though he called out the fellows' own names, they knew the somewhat trivial tokens had not been hand-picked especially for them.

Once the gifts found their way into the proper hands, Bill left. Oh, sometimes one of the kids got a little raucous, but the older ones did a pretty good job of maintaining order. The boys swapped stuff around until they got what they needed; one guy can use only so many hairbrushes. They played a few games. Everybody blew off the steam they'd bottled up since Thanksgiving. Some of the little fellows cried. Then, they all went to bed. Except maybe for a particularly physical basketball game, Christmas morning was just another day. Hardly a perfect system, but it worked.

All in all, Bill made the most of a bad situation.

His youngsters would not find adoptive parents. Too old. Bill knew it. They knew it. Bobby Harrad's caustic comment minced few words. "We ain't going anywhere, Mr. B. Nobody wants used kids. So do us a favor. Don't spend time Christmas Eve tryin' to con us into thinkin' everything'll be okay."

The evening passed with quick and quiet mercy. Each boy got six or seven things from the churches. The books survived their traditional underwhelming reception, and Bill slipped out as unobtrusively as possible.

❧❧❧❧❧

"Hey guys! There's more stuff back here!" Lamar's squeaky voice quivered with excitement. "Look! Presents! They're way in the back under this blanket . . . and . . . and they got names on 'em."

Lamar almost pulled down the tree trying to drag out the two large mystery boxes full of gifts. By the time he'd extracted the second and himself from the scraggly pine, the other boys were already grabbing packages and pushing them into one another's faces as fast as they could get them.

"Frank, here!"

"Louie! Hey, you got a big one!"

"John! Sam! Ronnie!"

And so it went, until each one of the seventeen clutched one last gift. For a while, they just sat there, unsure. Even though they could barely stand it, the younger ones waited, too. No use getting rapped on the noodle for messing up the routine. Everyone knew the rule: oldest first. For everything. But the veterans had never seen anything like this before.

"Must be from 'the Old Man,'" Ralph suggested. "He knows our names."

"Naw, can't be," Matt protested. "He gave us the books already. How 'bout Mrs. Grizwald?"

"No way, man. She's too big into turkey dinners. Besides, at least one of us helped her all day."

Bobby threw a crumpled cup across the room at Matt. "Who cares?" he snarled. "Let's just open the stuff and go to bed."

One of the little ones perked up. "All at once? What'll we do?"

Everyone turned to Sam. Although the second in age, Sam had assumed the leader's position for about the last year or so.

"Same as always, guys. We'll do it same as always. Bobby, you first. You're senior. Then me, Ralph, and on down . . . all the way to Jerome."

Jerome opened his mouth to protest, thought better of it, and shrugged in agreement.

Sam looked back. "Okay, Bobby, go on."

Bobby unwrapped the box with all the enthusiasm he applied to any other situation, so the unveiling dragged on for a while. Everybody knew he took his time to see if he could irritate someone, but the kids had long since quit giving him the satisfaction of knowing he could gig them. Finally, Bobby held up a heap of white toilet paper.

"Look," he mocked, "White Cloud. So soft and fluffy."

"Come on, jerk!" Sam's patience slammed shut. "Open it."

Bobby pried the tissue apart like avocado leaves, smoothed it out, and sat back. "Yippee! A basket."

That's what it was—a little basket, seven, maybe eight inches long. Bobby shook his head. "A basket made of weeds. Great gift, guys."

"What's that stuff called?" someone asked from the back. "Didn't we mess around with it before?"

"Yeah," Bobby sneered, "straw stringing or something. Remember the 'do-gooder' from the rec center this summer? Came to teach us. You know, 'Join the Farm—learn a trade.'"

Sam kept his voice level. "It's called wheat weaving, Bobby, and you know it. The lady was nice and it was fun."

"Yeah, somebody got into it in a big way, and I got this precious little basket." Bobby's face surrendered little zeal for his gift.

"Okay," Sam said. "Now mine."

The package denuding took considerably less time, and Sam held up the contents.

"What is it, guys? A cactus? No, it's a tree."

"Oh, the Mad Wheat Weaver strikes again." Bobby seldom let up once he got started. "Maybe Ralph got a monkey or some bananas. There's a thought—wheat-weaved bananas—high in potassium and fiber."

"Can it, Bobby! Okay, Ralph."

"Mine's a man. Well, maybe not. No, it's a boy. He's sort of short. A boy."

By now, everyone had managed to inch off most of the wrapping, so the inhabitants of the boxes appeared in rapid succession.

"Rocky?"

"I'm not sure. A man, I think. It's taller than Ralph's. Some sort of a super guy, maybe. You know, a cartoon character. See the cape. Faster than a speeding bullet. More powerful than Mrs. Grizwald's meatloaf. *Voom! Shazaam!*"

On they went, each of the boys' packages revealing yet another little wheat-woven creation, most of which defied accurate description. Robert was explaining his airplane when Sam hollered, "Wait! Wait a minute! I got it! You know what this is? Look. I got a tree. So did you and you. That's not a goat, Joey. It's a sheep. And that one's not a horse. Because of the hump, man. It's a camel.

"The guys with the capes and the glitter on their heads—kings with crowns. The real tall dude, and the little short one with the blue miniskirt—Joseph and Mary. Don't you get it? Bobby, that's not a basket.

"Who's got a present left?"

Jerome looked bug-eyed at his box. True to the rules, and very mindful of his lowly status as the youngest, Jerome hadn't disturbed so much as a piece of tape. He sat on the edge of a table, his hands nervously drumming a brightly colored package.

"Go on, Jerome," Sam prodded. "And, Bobby, shut up!"

Jerome gingerly pulled off the paper. He removed the lid, placed it to one side, reached into the box, and gently lifted out a little figure.

"Jesus!" Not an oath, but a gasp of reverence. "It's Jesus."

Jerome cupped the little straw Savior in his hands as if he carried the last few drops of water in the world, walked across the floor, and feathered it into Bobby's basket. One by one, the boys took their figures and arranged them around the tiny bed.

Mary, Joseph, shepherd, sheep, sages from the East, camels, trees, and an angel shaped like an airplane soon stood guard around baby and basket.

Sam finally broke the silence. "Y'all remember the program we did at that church? Remember that dorky song at the end—the one Mrs. Grizwald liked so much? Anybody know it?"

Danny started. He had the best voice. But pretty soon the majority of the boys sang along:

> Once in royal David's city
> Stood a lowly cattle shed,
> Where a mother laid her Baby
> In a manger for his bed;
> Mary was that mother mild,
> Jesus Christ, her little Child.
>
> And our eyes at last shall see Him,
> Through His own redeeming love;
> For that Child so dear and gentle
> Is the Lord of heaven above,
> And He leads His children on
> To the place where He is gone.

The boys felt warm and uncomfortable all at the same time. Those few kids who'd ever experienced a family celebration could not remember it, and Mrs. Grizwald had long ago deserted the idea of inflicting this head-bashing brood on any church's Christmas Eve service. No one prayed. No one preached. No one even recited the Christmas story from Luke. But for a moment, the insults stopped, the bitter loneliness subsided, and the bravado of wounded adolescence melted in the face of the white-hot blaze of worship.

Some of the boys held hands. Some draped their arms over a neighbor's shoulder. Most simply stood in the tight semicircle. But every single citizen of The Farm zeroed in on Magi, manger, and The Miracle.

They sang carols into the wee hours, one by one yawning and shuffling off to the dorm, until the group dwindled into nonexistence.

Daybreak began to consider crawling over the wall of the horizon, and still Bobby stood in front of the crèche: little straw animals and people bathed in the glow of the tree lights—each boy's individual present joining with the others to form the story and substance of that first night when angels sang and shepherds quaked.

Bobby shut off the tree, bent over the miniature scene, and spoke softly, "Guess you know what it's like to be away from home, huh, little guy? Well, merry Christmas anyway."

As he turned to leave, he shoved his fingers deep into the pockets of his overcoat and froze.

He looked right—left—back to the right. After checking one more time, he slouched about as quickly as he ever did over to the trash can, pulled out his left hand, and dropped in a slender stalk of dried wheat, the single remaining evidence of his gift.

One last look at the nativity scene that had finally given the only family he knew any sense of the joy and peace of the Season. Then, Bobby zipped up his coat and walked out into the cold dawn, singing the dorky little tune Mrs. Grizwald never knew he had learned.

What a Christmas!

"*C*hristmas—who needs it?*"

When the picture fell off the wall at the other end of the room, I glared at it as if it had done something other than what you would expect from a picture struck by a thrown shoe. After more than a few seconds of glowering, I sulked across the floor, like a child reluctantly trudging to take a bath, and inspected the damage.

The glass had remained intact, the shock of hitting the floor cushioned, no doubt, by the carpet, and though the frame looked a little nicked on one edge, by and large, the picture had withstood the plummet fairly well. The previously flung Weejun, lying on its guilty side, slid back over my toes without a whimper, none the worse for its aerial trip across the room.

What triggered the footwear bombardment I couldn't pinpoint with any certainty, but the explosion had been building for some time.

All day long, I could feel my inner temperature rising like some heat-seeking missile. My demeanor wore the scaly skin of antagonism, and I knew I was just putting off the detonation until a more opportune moment.

This December seemed pretty much the same as all the rest—at least at the beginning. I'd passed the Season with the same frantic efficiency I've exhibited every year since coming in off the road. Funny—it feels like only yesterday I was driving two, three, four hundred miles a day. And always the maniacal sprint home on Christmas Eve.

What had it been? Good heavens—five years as senior vice president in charge of distribution. I spent all day making sure other folks

> hit the bricks,
>> ran like rabbits,
>>> toted the load,
>>>> paid their dues.

Long time. Now, the new job didn't seem so special. The pay increases did not seem so special. This year, even Christmas Eve did not seem so special.

Gosh, what it used to be like. Make that last call about two o'clock in the afternoon, and always in some god-forsaken-out-of-the-way-no-name bubble of a town. But, no big deal. It was Christmas Eve. Even the most urgently needed visit collided with smiling faces and warm greetings. Sure, people had things to do—the world simply can't stop anymore just because of a holiday—and sometimes I could sense the pressure they carried, but they were always friendly and glad to see me.

And every single year, even the pickiest of customers eventually looked at the clock, shoved a cup of hot chocolate or Russian tea into my hand, and shooed me out the door: "Go on, we'll get the rest of the bugs out of the system next time you're around. It's Christmas Eve and it's getting late. You need to be on your way home. Scat!"

Off I'd dart, always taking a little extra care— no use ruining my Christmas and someone else's with a foolish fender bender, or worse. But, I mean to tell you, I drove hard. No stops, no soft drinks, just straight through—usually at least five hours. But I almost always managed to make it home in time to go to church with the family.

Man alive, I loved that stuff. I'd drag home absolutely dead to the world and within fifteen minutes of walking through the door, everyone had me so jazzed up I could have gone on for hours. Christmas Eve with the family,

> —unpacking cardboard boxes bearing goodies from the ones who couldn't make it this year,
> —divvying up all the presents and kidding whoever got the most about "Striking it rich!";
> —sipping cider and munching several dozen more cookies than twice as many folk should have eaten, but living in the complete assurance anything consumed in the festive spirit of Christmas Eve held neither consequence nor calories;
> —singing carols, telling stories everyone already knew by heart but tolerated again anyway, catching up, taking care;

—sitting in a darkened sanctuary, hearing the age-old story read again in all its powerful newness, and listening to the choir lilt: "What is this lovely fragrance wafting like to the scents of flowers in spring!"

Wonderful traditions, wonderful memories, and, tonight, they might as well have been tales from the Brothers Grimm.

On my return trip across the room, I looked for the cat to kick, realized we hadn't had a cat in years and that I wouldn't have abused one even if available, so I just slumped down in my fireside easy chair and prepared for an evening of self-pity.

Time alters a lot of things. Children grow up, leave home, get married, have children of their own. That's the way it's supposed to happen. But why do the holidays have to change? Why do the kids have to visit with in-laws or study abroad or decide to take trips? Of all times of the year, why would anyone take a trip at Christmas?

Don't they remember what it was like? Don't they know how important some things are? Why do they all have to be gone at once? It's not like they don't know their Grandmother's sick and their mother had to leave me and go to be with her. First time ever she and I haven't spent Christmas together. I understand that, but one of the kids could have changed something. Doesn't anyone care I'm here by myself?

Pain shot up my elbow. As if from another body, I looked down at the battered arm of the chair and watched as I began to rub my bruised hand. Then, the dam broke: "This isn't right! I've always made sure I was here for them! I'm all alone. This isn't Christmas! I'm all alone . . . "

The evening oozed along. Every time I looked at the clock I was sure someone had tampered with the hands, moving them backwards—nothing could possibly crawl by so slowly.

After a while—I really can't tell you how long—I got up and wandered around . . .

Went into all the kids' old rooms, maybe just to see if one of them had come,

Picked out a few sad, minor chords on the piano—by this time, I had the poor-pitiful-me routine mastered,

Straightened this candle, picked up that stray piece of paper.

The antique rolltop desk had been a gift from the family many years ago and was an office away from the office. No one, but no one, touched anything on my desk. It served as study, communications center, candy store, family museum and, with its multiplicity of nooks and crannies, even as a hiding place for very small but very special gifts.

I sat for a while, sorted through various papers and reports, then turned my attention to the day's mail. Not much, really. The folks who traditionally sent us a card got them to us plenty early, so most of the stack consisted of advertising flyers, promotional brochures, catalogs, and bills.

Most, but not all.

At the bottom of the pile, I found a white envelope bearing only my first name and my address. I'd seen the familiar, printed handwriting before—once a year, every Christmas—ever since a snowy Christmas Eve ten years ago. I didn't even have to look at the return address to know the upper-left-hand corner bore the initials J.J.T.

⁂

Suddenly, I found myself back there, in a small but cozy dwelling, a house made into a home by the warmth and love of a father, a mother, and their mentally handicapped son.

Ten years ago, like tonight, I'd been alone.

Ten years ago, on a miserable, snow-whipped Christmas Eve, Jake, Anna, and Jo-Jo Trimble had opened their door and their hearts to a stranger—to me.

Ten years ago, I'd carried home Jo-Jo's hand-made manger as a gift and as a reminder of the time long, long past when "righteousness and peace kissed one another."

I slit open the envelope and withdrew the card. The outside held no great promise. It was a generic card, a generic Christmas scene: two adults, one male, one female, huddled at the door of their little cottage, waving and listening to a trio of youthful carolers.

Jo-Jo sends me a card every year. I've rather come to take them for granted. Oh sure, I display them on the piano with the others, and when his comes, I usually take a moment to dust off the manger, which still sits on the mantel, but in all honesty, after a while, even Jo-Jo's greetings blend in with all the rest.

I gave the card a cursory glance and started to flip it to the corner of the desk when I realized it contained a message. On the inside of the upper fold, in Jo-Jo's very distinctive print, stood a strange and wonderful greeting. As I read it, I could hear Jo-Jo's innocent and eager voice:

WAY UP AT DARK COUNTRY ALASKA IT IS A ICE BOX AND NORTHERN LIGHT IS DOING DISPLAY IN THE NIGHT SKY AND HEAD WAY TO SOUTH OF PACIFIC OCEAN TO HAWAII THAT GIANT WAVE SURFING SANDY BEACHES HIGH FALL AT THE RIVER LIKE COOL SUMMER ON CHRISTMAS GOOD PINEAPPLE FEILD WITH SUGAR CANE FEILD AND CORN FEILD AND NEW YORK THEY ALL THRONG IN TO ST PATRICK CATHEDRAL AND ST JOHN THE DIVINE CATHEDRAL FOR MIDNIGHT MASS WHAT A CHRISTMAS THAT IS

HAVE A BIG MERRY CHRISTMAS

AND BIG NEW YEAR OF HAPPINESS JIMMY

The soothing words slowly lubricated my soul. I read and reread the devastatingly simple message, unsure of its exact meaning, but slowly, very slowly, catching the essence of the salutation.

From "way up north" all the way to the "giant wave," which Jo-Jo had never actually witnessed but could see with all his heart, everywhere from the frigid "icebox" to the "sandy beaches," from fields of rich and ripening fruit to the asphalt shores of the mightiest of cities, in every land, in every tongue, in every conceivable place, in Jo-Jo's mind, it was Christmas.

And even in the froth and bother of the metropolis, that young man understood a time would come when all people—young and old, the richly dressed and those clothed in someone else's castaways—would seek out a place so they could kneel before the wooden throne.

Oh, if we could all just see it, too. What if—in one magnificent, panoramic vision like the one held by this special child of God—what if we could all simultaneously glimpse every reach and region of our icebox, sandy beach world coming together with the shout:

O Come, let us adore Him!
Christs, the Lord!

By the time I was ready to leave for the church, the solitude seemed lighter. Oh, very little had actually changed, and I fully understood the morning would wander in with disturbing silence. But I also recognized my receipt of a great gift.

On my way to the door, I set the card next to the manger—a little, replicated feed box that had taken on a fuller, richer meaning.

"What a Christmas that is, Jo-Jo," I mumbled. "What a Christmas that is."

This story was inspired by a Christmas card sent to the author by Jimmy Parham, a very special friend and a very special child of Christmas.